W9-BDN-020

Plants

Kathryn Williams

NATIONAL GEOGRAPHIC

Washington, D.C.

How to Use This Book

Reading together is fun! When older and younger readers share the experience, it opens the door to new learning. As you read together, talk about what you learn.

This side is for a parent, older sibling, or older friend. Before reading each page, take a look at the words and pictures. Talk about what you see. Point out words that might be hard for the younger reader.

This side is for the younger reader.

As you read, look for the bolded words. Talk about them before you read. In each chapter, the bolded words are:
Chapter 1: places • Chapter 2: action words
Chapter 3: nouns • Chapter 4: describing words

At the end of each chapter, do the activity together.

Table of Contents

Plants Everywhere

YOU READ

Look around! There are plants everywhere. In the **city**, they live in flowerpots and parks. Some plants even grow through cracks in the sidewalk.

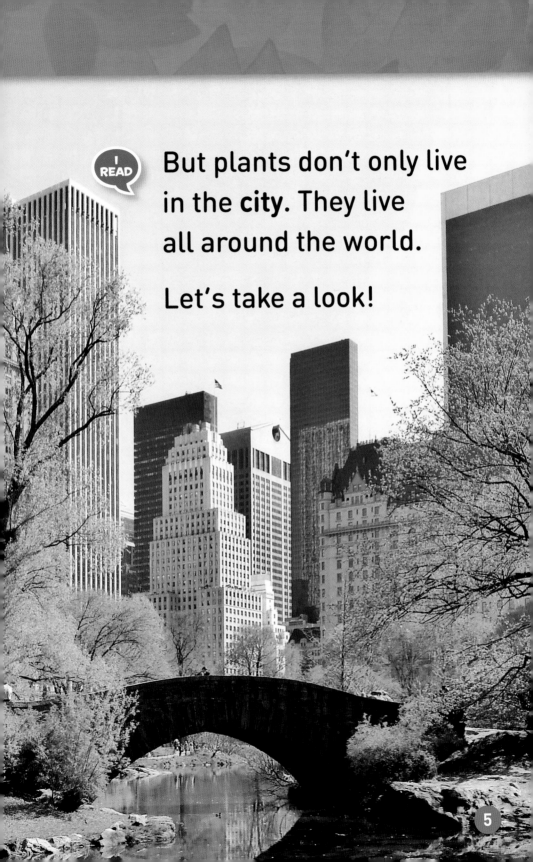

I READ But plants don't only live in the **city**. They live all around the world.

Let's take a look!

YOU READ

Many amazing plants, like kapok (KAY-pock) trees, live in the **rain forest**. Kapok trees can grow to be as tall as a 20-story building! They tower above the canopy, or treetops. That means they get lots of sunlight. Other plants grow in their shade.

Many orchids grow on other plants.

 This orchid (OR-kid) lives in the **rain forest**, too. It does not need much light. It grows in the kapok tree's shade.

YOU READ

Some plants live in the **water**. Sea grass grows in shallow ocean water, where there is plenty of sunlight.

These underwater meadows are home to lots of ocean animals, like fish and crabs. For green sea turtles, sea grass is a yummy snack!

 Other plants live in ponds.

This lily sits on top of the **water**. It has wide leaves to help it float.

YOU READ

The **desert** is a tough place for plants to grow. It is too dry for most plants to live there. But some cacti can live two years without any water. They have special parts to keep them cool and wet.

Spiky needles shade cacti from the sun. Waxy skin keeps water inside.

Life in the **desert** is easy for cacti! Like all plants, they have special ways to live in their home.

YOUR TURN!

These plants are out of place. Help them find their homes! Use your finger to draw a line from each plant to the place it lives.

C cactus

A orchid

B lily

1 desert

2 rain forest

3 pond

13

CHAPTER 2

What Is a Plant?

 Most plants don't move very much. They don't run or play. But all plants are living things. That's because they **grow** and change just like you do.

 All plants need things to live. They need space to **grow**. They also need food.

YOU READ

Plants can't go to the store and buy a sandwich. Instead, they make their own food from sunlight, water, air, and nutrients. They have special body parts to help them **gather** these ingredients.

Leaves **gather** sunlight and air. Wider leaves get more light. Flat leaves gather more light, too.

17

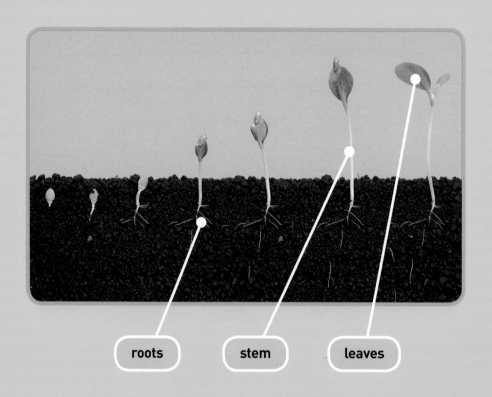

roots · stem · leaves

Roots help plants absorb water and nutrients. They usually grow down into the soil and spread out wide. Spreading out helps the roots collect more water. It also **holds** plants in place.

The stem carries water from the roots to the leaves. It also **holds** the

 YOU READ

All the parts of a plant work together to keep the plant healthy. Most plants have similar parts, but others are different.

Trees have big stems called trunks. Tough bark **covers** their trunks and keeps them safe.

Duckweed is made of lots of tiny plants.

 Duckweed has no stem at all. The plants **cover** the water like a big blanket.

YOU READ The Venus flytrap is a strange plant. It doesn't only get food from sunlight, water, and air. It gets the extra nutrients it **needs** from bugs! When an insect lands on a leaf, the leaf closes shut. The bug is trapped!

The Venus flytrap may be different, but it is still a plant.

It still makes its own food. And it still **needs** space to grow.

Just like other plants, its body parts all work together to help it live.

YOUR TURN!

There are all kinds of plants. Some have roots that go deep underground. Others have roots that stay close to the surface. Some have big leaves, and some have no leaves at all.

There's something strange about this plant. What's wrong with it? Do you think it would be able to grow? Why or why not?

Plants Grow Up

pod

seeds

Most plants start their lives as seeds. At first, they live inside or on their parent plants. Plants keep their seeds in different places. Some plants keep their seeds in **pods**, or protective cases.

Not all plants have **pods**. Some keep their seeds in fruits. Many fruits have seeds on the inside. Strawberry seeds are on the outside.

papaya

strawberry

apple

dandelion

maple seeds

YOU READ

When the seeds are ripe, it's time for them to leave their parent plants. They need their own space to grow.

Seeds have many ways of traveling to their new **homes**. Some seeds use the wind. Dandelion seeds float from one place to another. Maple seeds twirl like helicopters!

Burr pods often get a ride. They stick to animals that walk by. The animals drop them off at their new **homes**.

burr

Soon, the seeds fall to the ground. Now each has its own space. It is ready to grow into a plant.

First, the seed splits open. Then, the new plant's roots push down into the **soil**.

shoot

The roots grow long. They gather water. The plant's shoot grows up out of the **soil**. The plant grows taller and stronger.

Many plants will also grow flowers.
Flowers help make new seeds
by creating **pollen**, a powder that
travels from one flower to another.

Flowers attract insects with their
smells and bright colors.
Pollen sticks to the insects.

 Bees fly from one flower to the next. They leave **pollen** behind.

bean plant

 YOU READ Once a plant has new pollen, it can create seeds. That's why, without bees and other pollinators (POLL-ih-NAY-torz), it would be hard for some plants to grow. They are an important part of plants' life **cycles**.

Now the plant loses its flowers. New seeds grow, and the **cycle** starts over!

YOUR TURN!

These seeds are ready to travel to their new homes! How do you think each seed will get there? Take a look at this backyard. How many ways to travel can you see?

maple seeds

dandelion seeds

burrs

ANSWER: The maple and dandelion seeds could float on the wind. The burrs could stick to the dog or people.

37

CHAPTER 4

Plants and You

 Plants are all over the world, and that's a really good thing. Plants don't just sit around and look nice. They also keep you **healthy** and make people's lives better.

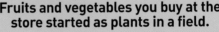
Fruits and vegetables you buy at the store started as plants in a field.

READ Fruits and vegetables are **healthy** snacks. You can pick them from a field and eat them.

YOU READ

Other plants help us make **tasty** foods that don't look like plants at all. Tortillas (tor-TEE-yuhs) are made of corn that has been cooked, ground up, and flattened.

READ Many **tasty** cakes are made with wheat.

Wheat and corn are both kinds of grasses.

Plants make up many of the **useful** things we see every day. Even some of our clothes used to be plants!

Cotton is the fluffy material that surrounds cotton plant seeds. Lots of pants and T-shirts are made with cotton.

 Wood is very **useful.**
People make toys, chairs
and tables, and houses
out of wood.

YOU READ

By simply growing, plants make the air that we breathe **clean**. Plants absorb parts of the air that we don't breathe and turn them into the oxygen that we need to live.

Plants make our world healthy and **clean**. That's why we need to take care of them.

YOUR TURN!

Look around! How many things can you find that are made from plants? How many of those things do you use every day?

For my dad —K.M.W.

Art Director: Amanda Larsen

The publisher and author gratefully acknowledge the expert literacy review by Kimberly Gillow, principal, Milan Area Schools, Michigan.

Library of Congress Cataloging-in-Publication Data

Names: Williams, Kathryn (Kathryn Marie), author.
Title: Plants / by Kathryn Williams.
Other titles: National Geographic kids readers. Level 1.
Description: Washington, D.C. : National Geographic Kids, 2017. | Series: National Geographic kids readers
Identifiers: LCCN 2016030944| ISBN 9781426326943 (pbk. : alk. paper) | ISBN 9781426326950 (library binding : alk. paper)
Subjects: LCSH: Plants--Juvenile literature.
Classification: LCC QK49 .W552 2017 | DDC 581--dc23
LC record available at https://lccn.loc.gov/2016030944

Illustration Credits
ASP = Alamy Stock Photo; GI = Getty Images; MP = Minden Pictures; SS = Shutterstock
Cover (CTR), Vladyslav Siaber/ASP; 1 (CTR), Anne Green-Armytage/GI; 3 (LO), BMJ/SS; 4 (UP), Arata Photography/GI; 4 (LO), Lorraine Boogich/GI; 5 (CTR), Cityscape_NYC/GI; 6 (UP), imageBROKER/ASP; 7 (CTR), Nick Garbutt/MP; 8 (UP), Reinhard Dirscherl/MP; 8 (LO), Borut Furian/GI; 9 (UP), Alex Huizinga/MP; 10 (CTR), Design Pics/Kristy-Anne Glubish/GI; 11 (CTR), Jacky946/GI; 12 (LO), Anneka/SS; 12 (CTR), Nella/SS; 12 (RT), arka38/SS; 13 (UP), gkuna/SS; 13 (CTR), 2009fotofriends/SS; 13 (LO), crotonoil/SS; 14 (LO), Frans Lanting/GI; 15 (UP), Christina Pudwill/EyeEm/GI; 15 (LO), Scorpp/GI; 16-17 (CTR), Takeshi.K/GI; 17 (CTR), Serg Myshkovsky/GI; 18 (UP), Redmal/GI; 19 (CTR), Stuart Minzey/GI; 20 (CTR), Lukiyanova Natalia/frenta/SS; 20 (LO), Jimcloughlin/GI; 21 (UP LE), Behindlens/GI; 21 (CTR), Jamie Felton/GI; 22 (LO), blickwinkel/ASP; 23 (UP), Lovleah/GI; 25 (CTR), Leonello Calvetti/GI; 26 (UP), Ed Reschke/GI; 27 (LE), Viktar Malyshchyts/SS; 27 (LO), Anna Kucherova/GI; 27 (RT), Tatiana Volgutova/GI; 28 (UP), Thomaslenne/GI; 28 (LO), stargatechris/ASP; 29 (UP), Simon-THGolfer/GI; 29 (LO), Wayne Hutchinson/MP; 30 (LO), JTB MEDIA CREATION, Inc./ASP; 31 (UP), Michael P Gadomski/GI; 32 (CTR), kenjii/SS; 33 (UP), Takeshi.K/GI; 33 (CTR), Fergus Gil/Nature Picture Library; 34 (UP), Mohamed Usman/EyeEm/GI; 35 (LO), oksana2010/SS; 36 (UP LE), Lisa J Goodman/GI; 36 (UP RT), sebastianosecondi/GI; 36 (LO), Aiv1112/GI; 37 (CTR), Mvailgursky/GI; 38 (LE), Ariel Skelley/GI; 38 (CTR), Tim Robbins/GI; 39 (UP), Monashee Frantz/GI; 40 (UP), Daniela White Images/GI; 40 (LO), Elena Grigarchuk/GI; 41 (UP), Jamie Grill/GI; 41 (LO), Erik Isakson/GI; 42 (LO), Australian Scenics/GI; 42 (CTR), AE Pictures Inc./GI; 43 (UP), Wdeon/GI; 43 (LO), Andy Crawford/GI; 44 (UP), Sky Matthews/GI; 45 (CTR), Lori Adamski Peek/GI; 45 (LO), Ariel Skelley/GI; 46 (xylophone), PlumpDi/Dreamstime; (pomegranate), NinaM/SS; (kiwi), NinaM/SS; (watermelon), NinaM/SS; 47 (blue jeans), Fync/Dreamstime; (wood blocks), Ewais/SS; (wood stool), Tatiana Popova/SS

National Geographic supports K–12 educators with ELA Common Core Resources. Visit natgeoed.org/commoncore for more information.

Printed in the United States of America
17/WOR/2